Introduction to

Living in the
Balance of
Grace & Faith

Andrew Wommack

© Copyright 2024 – Andrew Wommack

Printed in the United States of America. All rights reserved. No portion of this book may be reproduced, stored in a retrieval system, or transmitted in any form or by any means—electronic, mechanical, photocopy, recording, scanning, or other—except for brief quotations in critical reviews or articles, without the prior written permission of the publisher.

Unless otherwise indicated, all Scripture quotations are taken from the King James Version® of the Bible. Copyright © by the British Crown. Public domain.

Scripture taken from the New King James Version®. Copyright © 1982 by Thomas Nelson. Used by permission. All rights reserved.

All emphasis within Scripture quotations is the author's own.

Published in partnership between Andrew Wommack Ministries and Harrison House Publishers.

Woodland Park, CO 80863 – Shippensburg, PA 17257

ISBN 13 TP: 978-1-59548-706-3

For Worldwide Distribution, Printed in the USA

1 2 3 4 5 6 / 27 26 25 24

Contents

Introduction 1

Chapter 1 Grace and Faith 3
Chapter 2 God's Already Done It! 11
Chapter 3 Deep Dive into Ephesians 1
 – Part I 17
Chapter 4 Deep Dive into Ephesians 1
 – Part II 27
Chapter 5 As You Have Received Christ 35
Chapter 6 The Sabbath Rest 39
Chapter 7 Humility 45

Conclusion 51

Receive Jesus as Your Savior 53

Receive the Holy Spirit 55

Call for Prayer 57

About the Author 58

Introduction

Have you ever struggled to receive from God and wondered what you were doing wrong? Does your closeness to Him seem to fluctuate based on your behavior? Many Christians answer 'yes' to one or both questions because they don't understand what God has done for us. Some have become hopeless, thinking that the Christian life will never get better. Well, the good news is that there is something better. You've just got to learn how God intended you to live!

As I travel and minister, I often run into people dealing with challenges that frustrate them—how to receive healing, prosperity, or peace. When I hear them tell me how they're praying, the real problem becomes clear: They never learned to live in the balance of grace and faith. Because of that, they have difficulty receiving from and relating to God.

Walking in the balance of nearly anything can be a challenge. It can be like trying to walk on a tightrope: Leaning too heavily to one side or the other will cause you to fall. You may have been taught to put an emphasis on either grace or faith. But you'll never be able to thrive as a Christian if you don't learn how to walk in the balance between them.

There are many opinions on grace and faith, and that's one of the reasons we have so many denominations. Some Christians are in the grace camp and will say we're saved by grace alone. Christians in the faith camp will say we're saved by faith alone. Many people don't realize that Scripture teaches us to have a balance between grace and faith.

If this concept is new to you, this teaching will transform the way you think about grace and faith and will radically change your walk with God! At first, you may be shocked to learn what I'm going to say. You might be tempted to think that I'm just dealing with semantics. But what I'll share with you is foundational! Living in the balance of grace and faith is a normal part of the Christian life, and it's at the heart of what God has called me to teach. I want to encourage you to search these truths out in the Scriptures (Acts 17:11) and open your heart to receive, even if they are unfamiliar to you. I'm excited for what you're about to discover in the following pages!

Chapter 1

Grace and Faith

It's not wrong to say you're saved by grace. That's what the Bible says.

> ***For by grace are ye saved*** *through faith; and that not of yourselves:* it is *the gift of God: Not of works, lest any man should boast.*
>
> Ephesians 2:8-9 (emphasis added)

Grace is what God does in your life independent of you, and it was given to you *in spite of* who you are, not *because* of who you are. Grace provides everything Jesus purchased on the cross. That includes not just the initial born-again experience but everything that pertains to life and godliness—healing, prosperity, joy, and peace. You see, God has anticipated every need you will ever have, whether physical, financial, or emotional. You don't have to motivate God or get Him to do anything. He's already done it!

Some people think there are things you can do to get God to bless you. They are taught that God loves them proportional to their performance. But your "holiness" doesn't move God or make Him love you more. That's a misconception that has frustrated so many Christians. They say, "O God, I've been faithful, I've been serving You! Move in my life! I deserve Your favor!" They don't realize that what they've just done is try to earn a free gift.

> *But not as the offence, so also* is *the free gift. For if through the offence of one many be dead, much more the grace of God, and the gift by grace,* which *is by one man, Jesus Christ, hath abounded unto many.*
>
> Romans 5:15

Grace wouldn't be a gift if it wasn't free. This is a big deal. But what's important to reemphasize is that everything that comes by grace has already been provided. This takes the frustration out of the Christian life. How can you doubt that God will give you something if He *already* gave it?

Saved by Grace or by Faith?

I started off saying that grace saves, but it would be wrong to say that grace *alone* saves. If it did, then all would be saved because Scripture says,

For the grace of God that bringeth salvation hath appeared to all men.

Titus 2:11

God's grace is available to everyone, yet not everyone receives salvation.

The Lord is not slack concerning his promise, as some men count slackness; but is longsuffering to us-ward, not willing that any should perish, but that all should come to repentance.

2 Peter 3:9

That tells you it is God's will for every single person to be saved. Yet Jesus Himself said that there would be many more who will go by the broad gate unto destruction than who go by the narrow gate unto everlasting life (Matt. 7:13-14). That shows you that God's will does not automatically come to pass. In 1 John 2:2, it says that Jesus is the propitiation, or atoning sacrifice, for your sins, but not only for yours; He paid for the sins of the whole world. Jesus has made payment even for the sins of people who would reject Him. That further solidifies that grace is the same toward every person who has ever lived. It's not based on, or tied to, a person's performance; it is only based on what God did through Jesus Christ.

Now, even though grace is not based on your performance, some people have taken it too far. Under the guise of grace, they believe they have a license to sin and are promoting all kinds of things the Bible teaches against. That's an abuse of grace! A person who believes you can just go live in sin and that God approves of it needs to be born again. You are not saved by grace alone.

We can say that we were saved by grace to emphasize that we didn't save ourselves. I'm not going to nitpick. Before we were saved, we were so destitute that we had to have God come and save us. So, I understand that there are times to emphasize grace. However, it's also not wrong to say that you're saved by faith! Paul wrote,

> *Therefore we conclude that a man is justified by faith without the deeds of the law.*
>
> Romans 3:28

So, which is it: grace or faith? Technically, it's both! You are saved by grace through faith.

> *For by grace are ye saved through faith.*
>
> Ephesians 2:8a

We must have a balance between the two. Grace and truth came by Jesus Christ (John 1:17). God commended

His love toward us through Christ before we had ever done anything good or bad (Rom. 5:8). But the truth is, we need to understand how grace works *with* faith.

Faith that Appropriates

When I saw the balance of grace and faith—that grace is God's part and faith is our part—I understood that keeping these things in balance was not up to God but up to me. It's God who provides. It's His power, but it doesn't flow without our cooperation. And our faith doesn't force God to do anything. When we're living in the balance of grace and faith, we become a channel for God to flow through.

I want to share with you one of my definitions for faith, which took me twenty years to learn. Most people believe that faith is what you do to move God. But God isn't the one who's stuck. He doesn't have to move. Faith only appropriates (takes for your own use) what God has already provided by grace. Understanding this truth transformed my life!

Faith isn't something you do to move God; it's just your positive response to God, who has already moved. When your faith is in what Jesus has done for you rather than in what you are doing for Him, that is a whole new way to live.

It's Like Sodium Chloride

A man once came to me and said, "This reminds me of sodium chloride. By themselves, both sodium and chlorine are poisonous; they'll kill you. But if you mix them together, it makes sodium chloride, or table salt, which you can't live without." Grace and faith are like sodium and chlorine; you have to mix them.

Another way to think about this is that grace and faith are like two ditches on either side of a road. One ditch isn't better than the other. If you get stuck in either ditch, you're not going anywhere. That's how it is with grace and faith. You have to find the balance between the two.

If all you do is focus on grace, on what God has done, you will totally disconnect from responsibility for your actions. You'll get into laziness and complacency, and it'll lead you into an attitude of *que sera, sera*, "whatever will be, will be." It's an extreme sovereignty of God mentality to believe that everything that happens is ordained by God. That is not what the Word of God teaches. You have a part to play.

On the other hand, if all you do is focus on faith, you'll say, "Well, by faith, people were able to quench the violence of fire. They were able to stop the mouths of lions" (Heb. 11:33-35). Faith will become like a crowbar you use to pry blessings out of God. It will ultimately place the burden of salvation on you and be detrimental to your Christian life. When you do everything just right, then you're going to expect God to move on your behalf. That is totally wrong. That's not biblical faith. Faith is not something you do to get God to respond to you.

An overemphasis on faith will lead to what is called "works" or "legalism." It'll wear you out! I'll tell you, trying to twist God's arm to make Him do something is not an easy row to hoe. Nobody is up to that.

What I'm saying may already be striking a chord with you. You're praying and studying the Word. You're going to church. You're trying to live holy. You're doing everything you know, and you still aren't seeing the results that you want. It's like you're on a treadmill and you can't get off! Let me just encourage you that God loves you. He understands your frustration. That's why it's so important for you to *mix* grace and faith, or you'll end up in a ditch on one side of the road or the other. It's what I call 'saved but stuck'. If you want to get to your destination, you've got to stay in the middle of the road. This is also true when it comes to grace and faith.

Chapter 2

God's Already Done It!

You and God are in a partnership, and whatever He wants to accomplish in your life, He's going to need your cooperation to do it. Grace is God's part; faith is your part. If you understand that God has already done His part by giving you everything you need for life and godliness (2 Pet. 1:3), then all you need to do is positively respond by believing and receiving. It's really that simple. It's important to understand this in order to stay in the balance of grace and faith.

God, through Jesus, provided everything two thousand years ago. Before you and I existed, before our need existed, God already created the supply. You might say, "Where is it? I don't see anything." That's because it's in spiritual form in the spirit realm:

Blessed be *the God and Father of our Lord Jesus Christ, who hath blessed us with all spiritual blessings in heavenly* places *in Christ,*

Ephesians 1:3

God is not the one who determines whether the supply moves out of the spiritual realm and into the physical realm. That depends on you. When you believe God's Word, faith brings what He has already done out of the spiritual realm and into the physical realm.

If I told you that you had a million dollars buried in your backyard and you believed me, you'd go looking for it. If you had a huge backhoe or a bulldozer, you probably would find it quickly. If all you had was a teaspoon, it would take longer, but if you kept digging, you would find that million dollars. On the other hand, if you thought, *Well, I'm not sure there **is** a million dollars in my backyard. I can't see it. It would take too much effort to find out*, then that money would just sit there and never benefit you. However, if you knew beyond any shadow of a doubt that it was there, it would be just a matter of time until you found it.

This is what happened with me. I knew I was already blessed. If I would have thought, *I don't see anything, so it must not be there*, I wouldn't have had a successful Christian life. But I knew that God had already blessed me. That's what Ephesians 1:3 says. You've got to know that you've been blessed with all spiritual blessings in heavenly places. That's the unseen, spiritual realm. By faith, you reach over into the spirit realm and bring what's true, what's reality into the physical realm. Somebody may say, "Brother, you're weird. You're talking about things being real that you can't see. Isn't faith blind?" No, it isn't. Look at this verse out of Hebrews:

> *Now faith is the substance of things hoped for, the evidence of things not seen.*
>
> Hebrews 11:1

Faith is substance. It's real. The blessings of God exist; they're just unseen. Faith is how you bring them into physical manifestation. Remember, God has already done His part. What He's provided is a reality in the spiritual. That's grace. Your part is to respond by faith.

Faith Takes It

Let me share an example that I think will help you. When I was eight years old, I went to Vacation Bible School. There were about six hundred kids in this church, and I was on the very back row. A man was preaching and held up a dollar bill, which was a lot of money for a kid back then. The man said,

"I'll give this dollar bill to the first kid who comes up here and takes it." Immediately kids were all around him shouting, "I want it, I want it!" I thought, *Of all times to be sitting at the back of the church, this was the worst time!* However, this man just kept his arm up in the air, saying, "I'll give this dollar bill to the first kid who comes up here and takes it." Everybody was wondering, *What's he doing?* But he just kept repeating himself. About the third or the fourth time he said it, my lightning-fast mind understood what he was saying. I got out from the back row, ran down to the front of the church, pushed my way through all the other kids, and grabbed this guy's arm. I climbed up his side and snatched that dollar bill out of his hand!

When I did that, the man looked at me and said, "That is the first kid to come up here and take the dollar bill. All of you wanted it, but he took it." Then he used that illustration to teach that by grace, God provided everything. It's a free gift, but you can't just sit there and say, "Well, if God wants me to be saved, then I'll be saved." No, God has provided it, but you must reach out and take it by faith. You may be thinking, *How do I take it by faith?* Through renewing your mind.

Even if you're beginning to understand what I'm saying, there will probably still be some things that you believe God has provided by grace that you aren't seeing come to pass in your life. When that happens, you must keep renewing your mind with the Word of God:

> *And be not conformed to this world: but be ye transformed by the renewing of your mind, that ye may prove what* is *that good, and acceptable, and perfect, will of God.*
>
> Romans 12:2

The word "*prove*" here means to make manifest to the physical senses. As you renew your mind, what already exists in your spirit is able to flow through your mind and emotions and out into your physical body. What's in the spiritual realm will start to manifest in the physical realm. It's a process, but it works!

Chapter 3

Deep Dive into Ephesians 1 – Part I

The book of Ephesians is a great example of what I've been sharing with you so far. The first three chapters talk about what God has already done, independent of you, which is grace. Then chapters four through six talk about how you should respond to God's grace, which is faith. They include instructions on how to conduct yourself as a believer and how to treat your spouse and your children. Why? Because even though the grace of God is independent of you, you control the flow of grace in your life. Some people would say, "Well, it's all the grace of God." If that were so, then you could treat people any way you wanted, and it wouldn't matter because God's grace will work regardless. But that's not true. You play a part in how grace operates in your life. Scripture tells us that God resists the proud but gives grace to the humble (James 4:6 and 1 Pet. 5:5), you can frustrate the grace of God (Gal. 2:21), and even receive more grace (James 4:6). Everything God has provided through His grace is accessed through faith (Rom. 5:2), which means it takes your cooperation. It's just like God's provision of salvation. Through Jesus, forgiveness and acceptance are available, but it's up to you to believe and receive that you are forgiven and accepted.

Ephesians 1:6 says,

To the praise of the glory of his grace, wherein he hath made us accepted in the beloved.

Did you know that the word "*accepted*" used here in the Greek is only used one other time in Scripture, when the angel Gabriel told the Virgin Mary that she was highly favored of God (Luke 1:28)? That means that in the same way Mary, the mother of Jesus, was accepted, you also are accepted. You are highly favored of God. He loves you just as much as He loved Mary. A lot of people will think, *Well, yeah, God loved the Virgin Mary*, but they'll put themselves into another category. They struggle to believe that God could love them that much. But He does. You are accepted in the beloved!

Notice that "accepted" in Ephesians 1:6 is past tense. That means it's already done. Again, most people think that they have to live holy and perform for God in order to be accepted by Him. No, you're already accepted in Christ! It's a done deal. But it's not good enough just to accept this on an intellectual level—you've got to believe it in your heart. That's when what God has accomplished in the spirit will begin manifesting in the physical realm. Faith does not cause God to accept you, but rather your faith just receives what has already been given to you through Christ. That is the balance of grace and faith.

Redemption

A man came to one of my meetings where I preached these exact truths about grace and faith. He had been a Catholic in Central America, and he pulled up his sleeves and pant legs to show me many scars he'd gotten crawling over broken glass during Lent. He had believed that he needed to do penance and somehow try to earn forgiveness from God. Did you know that that is an insult to God? That's saying Jesus isn't enough, that you have to add to what He did in order to be forgiven. Most people wouldn't go to that extreme, but they essentially do the same thing when they fast, pray, and read the Word. Now, if you're fasting to humble yourself and make yourself more sensitive to God, that's fine. But if you're doing it to put pressure on God, to manipulate Him, that's just as offensive as crawling three miles over broken glass.

Ephesians 1:7 says,

In whom we have redemption through his blood, the forgiveness of sins, according to the riches of his grace.

This is not saying that if you will repent, then God redeems you. No, He's already redeemed you. The price has already been paid by the shed blood of Jesus. It's just a matter of whether you will believe and receive or if you'll doubt and do without. The only thing you can do is have faith in what Jesus has done. But if you start putting faith in what *you've* done, that's not biblical faith.

Already within You

Did you know that in your born-again spirit, you have all the wisdom of God? The Scripture says,

Wherein [God] hath abounded toward us in all wisdom and prudence.

Ephesians 1:8

This was a work of grace. Now, the Scripture also says,

If any of you lacks wisdom, let him ask of God, who gives to all liberally and without reproach, and it will be given to him.

James 1:5 NKJV

So, it is appropriate to ask for wisdom, but you aren't asking for the wisdom to come from the outside in; you're asking for the wisdom that you already have in your born-again spirit to come out and be made manifest to your physical mind. You might be thinking, *Why does it matter whether it comes from the outside or from the inside?* It matters because it's easier to release something that you already have than to go get something you don't have.

When I was in my poverty days, the Bible that I had with me through Vietnam was mildewed. Most of the pages were totally taped over. Entire chapters and books of the Bible had fallen out. I was pastoring a church and didn't even have a full Bible! I didn't have much money to get a new one either. So, I started believing God for the money to get a new Bible. This isn't an exaggeration: It took me a couple months to get an extra twenty dollars for a new Bible. During that time the devil was pounding me, saying, "Some man of God you are. You don't even have enough money to get a Bible! How can you pray for people to be saved and healed and delivered? It'll never work. You're a failure!" I dealt with doubt about that nearly every single day. But when I finally got the money, I bought the Bible and had my name engraved on it. When I walked out of that bookstore, I had that Bible in my hand, and I never doubted that I'd get it once I had it. You're probably thinking, *Well, of course! Why would you ever doubt you're going to get something if you've already got it?* That's my point. Once you have something, all the doubt about getting it leaves.

There is never going to be a question that comes up in your life that your born-again spirit doesn't already have the answer to. You just have to get it into your physical mind. That takes faith!

Ephesians 1:9 goes on to say,

Having made known unto us the mystery of his will, according to his good pleasure which he hath purposed in himself.

Get this: God already made known the mystery of His will to you. That's powerful! Colossians 1:27 says that this mystery is Christ in you, the hope of glory. The Holy Spirit has been dispatched and placed on the inside of you to reveal Jesus to you. That's His job. But it's not going to happen in your life without your participation. God wants Jesus to be revealed to you more than you want Him to be revealed, but you must spend time renewing your mind for this to happen. You can't waste all your time watching ungodly television shows and all the bad news in the media. You've got to spend time focusing on the Lord through the Word of God.

Continuing in Ephesians,

> *That in the dispensation of the fulness of times he might gather together in one all things in Christ, both which are in heaven, and which are on earth;* even *in him: In whom also we have obtained an inheritance, being predestinated according to the purpose of him who worketh all things after the counsel of his own will.*
>
> Ephesians 1:10-11

You already have your inheritance. It's *in* you! No one is completely manifesting the fullness of this, but the inheritance is complete. When you get born again, it's not like your spirit is in baby form, and then when you get to heaven, you're this complete person. No! Your spirit is not going to be changed. It's not going to be dusted off or injected with more power or anointing. Your spirit is as saved and as perfect right this second as it will ever be throughout eternity. It's full-grown and mature.

When you get to heaven, you will see and experience the fullness of your spirit. You'll get a glorified body that is no longer subject to the things of this life (1 Cor. 15:53-54). You will know all things even as you are known (1 Cor. 13:12) because you will receive a glorified soul. The former things won't even come to mind (Is. 65:17). Paul confirms this a few verses later, where he wrote,

Ye were sealed with that holy Spirit of promise, which is the earnest of our inheritance until the redemption of the purchased possession, unto the praise of his glory.

Ephesians 1:13b-14

The word "*earnest*" here is talking about a down payment. If you were going to buy a house, you would be asked for some earnest money to prove that you're serious. So, you'd put down a portion of that purchase price. Well, receiving this born-again spirit is God's down payment on your inheritance. Your spirit is complete, but it's only a portion of what you will receive. When you go to be with the Lord, then your soul and your body will be complete. In this life, to the degree that you renew your mind and act accordingly, you will manifest what's in your spirit.

I know that there are people who will say, "That's not true!" That's because they only believe what they see in the physical realm. If they can't see it or feel it, they doubt that it exists. However, the Scripture says,

he that is joined unto the Lord is one spirit [with Him]

1 Corinthians 6:17

and

ye are complete in him.

Colossians 2:10a

First John 4:17 says,

Herein is our love made perfect, that we may have boldness in the day of judgment: because as [Jesus] is, so are we in this world.

It didn't say, "so are you going to be in the next world"; It says you are as Jesus is right now. That's the resurrected Christ! You must believe that this is what God has provided by grace.

Ephesians 1:12-14 confirms this point, saying,

That we should be to the praise of his glory, who first trusted in Christ. In whom ye also trusted, *after that ye heard the word of truth, the gospel of your salvation: in whom also after that ye believed, ye were sealed with that holy Spirit of promise, which is the earnest of our inheritance until the redemption of the purchased possession, unto the praise of his glory.*

When you were born again, you were sealed with the Holy Spirit of promise. That means your spirit was vacuum-packed. When you sin as a Christian, that sin will not penetrate and contaminate your spirit. It will affect only your body and your soul. In other words, sin gives Satan an inroad into your life to afflict you with sickness, poverty, and depression. But your spirit will remain righteous and truly holy (Eph. 4:24).

Chapter 4

Deep Dive into Ephesians 1 – Part II

One of the reasons Paul saw so much victory in his life is because he understood this truth that God had provided everything by grace. A great example of this is his prayer for the church at Ephesus. Think about this: If you knew you were going to write a prayer for people two thousand years in advance, what would your prayer be like? I guarantee you, most people would write, "O God, send revival. Move in our lives. Do a new thing. Pour out Your Spirit again, for Jesus' sake. Amen." That would be a typical prayer, and it would be absolutely pathetic. But Paul's prayer was totally different. Look at the way he prayed:

Wherefore I also, after I heard of your faith in the Lord Jesus, and love unto all the saints, cease not to give thanks for you, making mention of you in my prayers;

that the God of our Lord Jesus Christ, the Father of glory, may give unto you the spirit of wisdom and revelation in the knowledge of him: the eyes of your understanding being enlightened; that ye may know what is the hope of his calling, and what the riches of the glory of his inheritance in the saints, and what is the exceeding greatness of his power to us-ward who believe, according to the working of his mighty power.

Ephesians 1:15-19

Paul's prayer wasn't, "God, do something new"; it was, "God, open their eyes and show them what You've already done!" Now, that's powerful. And that is the victory in the Christian life. The Bible says,

For whatsoever is born of God overcometh the world: and this is the victory that overcometh the world, even our faith"

1 John 5:4

You don't receive from God by trying to make Him heal you, bless you, or prosper you. Blessings come when you acknowledge that God has already provided these things by grace and then you receive them by faith. When you get your heart established and can say beyond a shadow of a doubt, "I'm blessed! I don't care what it looks like," that's when you start growing as a Christian. That's how you will release the blessing of God.

When you understand that, it changes the way you read the rest of the prayer Paul wrote. For instance, he asked that God would "*give unto you the spirit of wisdom and revelation in the knowledge of Him*" (Eph 1:17). Paul is not asking that this would come from an outside source. Rather, he's praying that the wisdom that's already in your born-again spirit would come out and start to influence your thinking and your actions.

Our faith becomes effectual (begins to work) by acknowledging what we already have in Christ Jesus (Philem. 1:6).

Understanding What it Means to be Enlightened

This same principle applies where Paul wrote that the eyes of your understanding would be enlightened. I don't have the space to dissect this completely here, but the word *understanding* in Ephesians 4:18 means deep thought. In other words, there are people who will say, "Oh, yeah, Jesus loves me," but they never really give it a second thought. They don't plumb the depths of it. Then there are others who have taken that statement, and it has become a heartfelt truth, not just superficial information. It's become experiential knowledge. That's what Paul was praying for you.

The word *enlightened* also in this verse is talking about having a revelation. This isn't just intellectual. You have to perceive these things from your heart. The Bible is not just written to your head; it's written to your heart. That's not to say that you should turn off your brain and quit thinking. No, you need to let the Holy Spirit, through your born-again spirit, enlighten your mind. You can see things clearer with your heart than you can see with your mind. That's an awesome truth.

Notice it also says that God's inheritance is in the saints (Eph. 1:18), but this inheritance isn't just waiting in heaven. The fullness of the inheritance won't be manifest until you get to heaven and get a glorified body and soul, but right now, you have the completeness of God in your born-again spirit. It's already been done as a work of grace.

Then Paul prays that you would have a revelation of the exceeding greatness of God's power toward you as a believer (Eph. 1:19a). Most people are saying, "O God, just give me more power!" They believe that God is almighty and can do anything, but they don't believe that He has given them anything. They want God to stretch forth His hand and heal them, but the Bible says, *"by whose stripes ye **were** healed"* (1

Pet. 2:24, emphasis added). They want God to bless them, but the Bible says they are *already* blessed (Eph. 1:3). They want God to prosper them, but the Bible says He has *already* given them power to get wealth (Deut. 8:18).

You have the same power that raised Jesus Christ from the dead on the inside of you (Eph. 1:19b-21). However, there are laws that govern how it works, just like there are laws that govern how electricity works. Electricity flows through copper better than it flows through wood. It doesn't matter if you like wood more than copper; if you try to wire your house with wood, it won't conduct that power. The same principle applies to the way God's power works. He is the one who established the spiritual laws, and you must discover and cooperate with them if they're going to work in your favor. For instance, God's power won't flow through unforgiveness, bitterness, or unbelief. They don't conduct the power of God. Does getting rid of unforgiveness and negative attitudes make God move? No. God has already generated the power by grace; all you need to do is use the right conductor, which is faith.

You can compare this concept to the way a television set works. Right now, there are multiple broadcast signals all around you. If you wanted to prove that there are signals to pick up, all you'd have to do is get a television set, plug it in, turn it on, and tune it in to one of the signals. The signal does not start broadcasting when you tune in. The television station was broadcasting before you turned on the set; you just started receiving the signal when you turned it on. In a similar way, God is constantly broadcasting everything by grace. It's already on the inside of you, but you must learn how to receive by faith what God has provided by grace.

Power Over the Devil

I talk to people all the time who beg me, "Please, help me overcome the devil." I just tell them, "You have the same power on the inside of you that raised Christ from the dead. That's more than enough to deal with the devil." You see, they've made the devil out to be a power greater than what they've got. Just because you may not be manifesting that power doesn't mean God didn't give it to you. You've just believed what religion has taught you. You're believing what the devil is telling you. Or maybe you're letting circumstances dictate what you believe to be true. The Bible says that God set Jesus

> *Far above all principality, and power, and might, and dominion, and every name that is named, not only in this world, but also in that which is to come: and hath put all things under his feet, and gave him to be the head over all things to the church, which is his body, the fulness of him that filleth all in all.*
>
> Ephesians 1:21-23

Even if you are the least member of the body of Christ, because you are in Christ, Satan is under you. You must believe what God's Word says. You already have everything that it takes to overcome. You resist the devil, and he will flee from you (James 4:7). God is waiting for you to stand up and believe. *You* have the authority! You must *know* in your heart that He has already given you all the power you need. Will you cooperate with it by faith?

Chapter 5

As You Have Received Christ

We were born again not when we were at our best but when we were at our worst. It says in Romans 5:8:

But God commendeth his love toward us, in that, while we were yet sinners, Christ died for us.

You didn't earn your salvation by fasting and praying, going to church, and paying your tithes. You were a total mess. You may think, "Oh, not me. I really was a good person." Well, if you think Jesus only added a little bit of righteousness to what you already had, I'm not sure you were ever born again. Jesus gave Himself for the ungodly (Rom. 4:5). You have to come to the end of yourself and realize that you're a sinner in order to qualify for salvation.

When there wasn't any goodness to your name, you received the greatest miracle you could ever receive. You might have been living in adultery, getting drunk, or doing dope, but you received by faith. In Colossians 2:6, the Apostle Paul wrote:

As ye have therefore received Christ Jesus the Lord, so walk ye in him.

That means that if you received the greatest gift of all—salvation—when you didn't have any goodness, then receiving by faith is the way you're supposed to continue to walk as a Christian. You started in faith, and you must continue in faith. But if you feel like you have to earn healing, prosperity, or anything else from God, you aren't walking by faith.

The Double Standards of Religion

Let's suppose somebody came forward for salvation at a church service, and God showed the pastor that they were living in adultery. If the pastor was to tell them, "You're living in adultery," that wouldn't stop them from getting saved. Why? Because, if they truly understood that they're saved by grace through faith, *not based on their goodness*, they would say, "Well, that's the reason I'm coming to Jesus. I need to be saved!"

Now, if that person got saved and started going to the average church, the people there would tell him, "Oh, yeah, you got saved by putting faith in what Jesus did. But now that you're born again, you've got to start living holy. If you don't come to church, pay your tithes, and follow our rules, God won't heal you or answer your prayers." That's a double standard. It's inconsistent with the way things worked at the beginning.

So many people have a honeymoon experience when they first get born again—all the colors become brighter, the sky gets bluer, the grass gets greener, and everything is just awesome. They're living in the balance of grace and faith almost effortlessly. But then they're told that they have to perform to *maintain* their salvation. This saps the life right out of them. That spark they once had with God begins to wane. They'll try to comply with all the rules they're given because they're so hungry, they're so eager to live for God. But after a time, they get worn out and wind up getting frustrated with the Christian life. They don't realize that they've moved away from grace and started putting faith in their performance.

That is the opposite of what Paul was talking about in Colossians 2:6. Since you were saved by grace through faith, that's the way you need to continue to walk! Paul wrote to Timothy,

Thou therefore, my son, be strong in the grace that is in Christ Jesus.

2 Timothy 2:1

I can tell you that the success I've experienced in my life and ministry is because I've learned to depend on the grace of God. It's not me. I'm just relying on what Jesus has done for me, not what I do for Jesus.

I've known religious people who were doing everything they knew to do, and yet they weren't seeing any of God's promises manifest. Then some drunk stumbles in off the street. He comes in, receives Jesus, and instantly gets delivered or healed. And instead of people rejoicing with him, their thought is, *Why did God do it for him and not for me? I've been serving the Lord for twenty years. I make pies for people. When people have a tragedy, I go over and help them. I'm at the church every time the doors are open. Why am I not healed?* I can tell you why. That old rank sinner heard the good news and just believed. He put total faith in Jesus, not in himself. The religious folks were putting faith in all their works or performance, trying to earn God's favor. That's legalism. You must put faith in what Jesus did if you're going to live in the balance of grace and faith.

Chapter 6

The Sabbath Rest

When the Lord rested on the seventh day after creation, it wasn't because He was worn out. He doesn't get tired. God rested because the work He had done in creation was so complete that He literally didn't have anything else to create. Now, as New Testament believers, we are to enter into His rest. We enter into what He has already provided by grace.

Did you know that God's intention has always been that His people enter His rest? The Israelites who came out of Egypt with Moses didn't enter into the Promised Land but spent forty years in the wilderness because they rebelled against God. It was self-inflicted. They just refused to obey God.

While it is said, To day if ye will hear his voice, harden not your hearts, as in the provocation. For some, when they had heard, did provoke: howbeit not all that came out of Egypt by Moses. But with whom was he grieved forty years? was it not with them that had sinned, whose carcases fell in the wilderness? And to whom sware he that they should not enter into his rest, but to them that believed not? So we see that they could not enter in because of unbelief.

Hebrews 3:15-19

God had planned something better for the Israelites than what they experienced. He'd provided them a Promised Land where He was going to get rid of the giants living there. The Israelites would have had homes built by giants. They were going to have fields that had already been cultivated and were fruitful. What a blessing! But the Israelites didn't enter in because of their unbelief.

The Scripture continues,

Let us therefore fear, lest, a promise being left us of entering into his rest, any of you should seem to come short of it.

Hebrew 4:1

The writer of Hebrews is using what happened to the Israelites as an example for us. We could be born again (delivered from Egypt) and yet not enter into all the blessings God has for us (rest) because of unbelief. The writer goes on to say,

> *For unto us was the gospel preached, as well as unto them: but the word preached did not profit them, not being mixed with faith in them that heard* it.
>
> Hebrews 4:2

That is one powerful statement! Did you know that you have to mix faith with the Word in order for it to release its power? The Bible shouldn't be treated like any other book that you just pick up and put down. It has the very words of God in it. His Word is designed to go into your heart, even as a seed is designed to be planted in the ground (Mark 4:3-20). That only happens when you read it with your heart and not just with your mind. Why? Because it's with the heart that man believes (Rom. 10:10), and if you're going to enter into God's rest, you've got to mix faith with His Word.

There Is a Rest for You

> *There remaineth therefore a rest to the people of God.*
>
> Hebrews 4:9

This Sabbath rest that the writer of Hebrews is talking about is comparable to Adam and Eve entering into God's rest after everything was created for them. All they had to do was reach out, partake of what He provided, and say thank you. Likewise, now that we are born again, there is a rest for us. Remember that when we were born again, God placed everything we will ever need on the inside of us. That's a concept very few Christians understand.

If a person gets sick, they know God can heal, but then they often start begging Him to heal them. They'll even say things like, "Stretch forth Your hand and heal me." God doesn't need to stretch forth His hand. As we've read, He placed the same power that raised Christ from the dead on the inside of us (Eph. 1:18-20). These Christians have not entered into God's rest. Instead, they are working and striving, trying to get God to do something He has already done. Again, that is not biblical faith.

The Sabbath was a shadow, a picture of the New Testament reality that God is our source (Col. 2:17). We need to recognize that even though we study the Word, go to church, and pay our tithes, it's not what we do that brings the increase; it's God's grace. All we're doing is responding to Him in faith.

Misconceptions about Rest

One of the things that causes people to misunderstand what the writer of Hebrews is talking about is the idea that rest only means lying down and doing nothing. However, if you keep reading, it says,

> *Let us labour therefore to enter into that rest.*
> Hebrews 4:11a

How can you labor to rest? It seems like a contradiction. But this is talking about putting all your confidence in what Jesus has done instead of what you are doing. It takes effort. It takes submitting yourself to God to get to the place where you are not looking to yourself as the source.

"Well, that sounds like works," someone will say. No, I'm not talking about works of the flesh or works of the Law. I'm talking about the kind of labor that causes you to simply trust that God has already provided everything. Going back to Hebrews 4:10, it says you must cease from your own works as God did from His. This is the Promised Land God has provided for you. This is grace. You can't add to it. All you can do is rest in what He has provided.

Chapter 7

Humility

Do you want to know another reason so many people are not seeing the grace of God, while others are walking in it? Look what the Apostle Peter wrote:

God resisteth the proud, and giveth grace to the humble.

1 Peter 5:5

That is one awesome statement. Was Peter saying God hates people, resists them, and is going to punish them? No, the grace of God is full of mercy. But grace is like electricity. It only flows through those who are humble. It's a spiritual law. If you're in pride and you're trying to walk in grace, there will be resistance. The power will not flow through you. Again, a lot of people have been taught that faith is like a crowbar. They think, *I'm going to make God heal me. I'm going to make God move.* That's nothing but pride, and God resists them.

Pride isn't limited to thinking that you're better than everybody else; that's only one manifestation of it. Being self-sufficient or self-dependent is also pride. When God calls someone and they get into pride, they start thinking, *God, You just introduce me, and I can handle it from there. I am so awesome! No wonder You called me!* This is a disaster waiting to happen.

No Confidence in the Flesh

Think of it this way: How can imperfect people represent and *re*-present a perfect God? You know you can't do it in your own strength. God hasn't had anyone qualified working for Him yet. The only way you can represent Him is to humble yourself and say, "It's not about me. It's all about You."

1 Corinthians 1:26-28 says,

For ye see your calling, brethren, how that not many wise men after the flesh, not many mighty, not many noble, are called: but God hath chosen the foolish things of the world to confound the wise; and God hath chosen the weak things of the world to confound the things which are mighty; and base things of the world, and things which are despised, hath God chosen, yea, and things which are not, to bring to nought things that are.

God doesn't call the qualified; He qualifies the called! Why? The next verse says He chooses the weak things so that no flesh will glory in His presence (1 Cor. 1:29). When God flows through somebody who is humble, He gets the glory. That is the way grace works, and we need to stop depending upon ourselves if God's grace is going to flow through us. Paul said he had "*no confidence in the flesh*" (Phil. 3:3). He went on to say,

> *But what things were gain to me, those I counted loss for Christ. Yea doubtless, and I count all things* but *loss for the excellency of the knowledge of Christ Jesus my Lord: for whom I have suffered the loss of all things, and do count them* but *dung, that I may win Christ, and be found in him, not having mine own righteousness, which is of the law, but that which is through the faith of Christ, the righteousness which is of God by faith.*
>
> Philippians 3:7-9

Here was the Apostle Paul, the most accomplished man of his day, and yet he walked in humility. He didn't have an inflated opinion of himself. But he knew that God had called him. He said,

> *But by the grace of God I am what I am: and his grace which was* bestowed *upon me was not in vain; but I*

laboured more abundantly than they all: yet not I, but the grace of God which was with me.

1 Cor. 15:10

That is powerful!

Humble Yourself

Some people wait until life humbles them before they ever say, "I've become so humble." No, if something was done to you that caused you to be humble, that's called humiliation. But humility is something you voluntarily do.

Humble yourselves therefore under the mighty hand of God, that he may exalt you in due time.

1 Peter 5:6

You need to humble *yourself* under the mighty hand of God if you're going to be exalted. Boy, that's a powerful point! Most people are looking to exalt themselves. They think that if they don't stand up for themselves and promote themselves, no one else will. But that isn't true. If you will humble yourself, God will exalt you in due time.If you've ever gotten angry at God, saying, "God, this isn't fair. How come I'm being treated this way? I did everything right. I've served You. You failed me," then you do not understand the role that humility plays in grace and faith. It's the old Job mentality, that God owes you something. Any person who has felt that way, I guarantee you, is one proud person. I'm not saying that to upset you; I'm saying it to show you how to properly relate to God. You need to humble yourself.

Casting All Your Cares

Did you know that one of the ways to discern whether you are humble or not is to determine whether you are casting your care on the Lord? That's the context of 1 Peter 5:7, which says,

Casting all your care upon him; for he careth for you.

Notice that Peter said this right after talking about humbling yourself. It's a completion of the thought. If you will humble yourself, then you won't have cares. That might be hard to believe, but that's what he is saying. When you realize that it's not about you, it can release you from carrying burdens. However, if you think you have to pray, you have to fast, and you have to stay up all night figuring things out, then I guarantee you'll have burdens because you'll be out of balance with grace. You'll be frustrating the grace of God because God gives grace to the humble.

A big part of humility is learning to cast all your cares upon the Lord. It's learning to trust that if He's called you to do something, then your only responsibility is to respond to

His ability. You do not have to figure everything out. Again, your spirit already knows what to do. It's not worried. It's not fretting. You just need to get your mind and emotions to agree with your spirit and cast your cares upon the Lord.

This is how I live. I had somebody ask me, "What are your goals?" Some people are so pressured by external things giving them purpose. But you can't even let good things cause you to have cares. I can honestly say that my goal in life is just to know the Lord and fellowship with Him. It's the only goal I've got. Of course, I've got plans for our ministry and our Bible college, and I believe the Lord has told me to do some things. But if nothing else worked in my life, I've still got a purpose, and I'd be happy whether anything else ever came to pass or not. I just want to know the Lord, and I believe that's a good place to be. I don't feel pressure or weight on me because my faith is not in all the things that I'm doing. My care is cast on Him, and I sleep well at night.

A lot of Christians can't say that because they're preoccupied with the cares of this world, the deceitfulness of riches, and the lusts of other things (Mark 4:19). But if you can learn to walk in humility and cast your cares upon the Lord, you'll realize that it's simple. God cares for you. You can go to sleep, trusting that by grace, He has provided everything that you need. Isn't that good news?

Conclusion

I pray that your eyes have been enlightened to see that everything has been provided by grace. Healing, prosperity, joy, peace, and the forgiveness of your sins are all blessings in heavenly places (Eph. 1:3). As you understand by now, grace alone doesn't save. By faith, you must appropriate what God has provided. It's like reaching over into the spiritual realm and bringing these blessings into physical manifestation. "*By grace you have been saved **through** faith*" (Eph. 2:8 NKJV). All you have to do is believe, receive, and labor to rest. That will take effort on your part—to simply trust that God has already provided everything and to partake of these things. But if you'll humble yourself, if you'll cast your care upon the Lord, then grace will abound toward you. You'll be living in the balance of grace and faith. This is how I relate to the Lord, and you can learn to relate to Him this way too. It's awesome!

FURTHER STUDY

If you enjoyed this booklet and would like to learn more about some of the things I've shared, I suggest my teachings:

- *Spirit, Soul & Body*
- *You've Already Got It!*
- *Plain as Dirt*
- *Effortless Change*

These teachings are available for free at **awmi.net**, or they can be purchased at **awmi.net/store**.

Receive Jesus as Your Savior

Choosing to receive Jesus Christ as your Lord and Savior is the most important decision you'll ever make!

God's Word promises, *"That if thou shalt confess with thy mouth the Lord Jesus, and shalt believe in thine heart that God hath raised him from the dead, thou shalt be saved. For with the heart man believeth unto righteousness; and with the mouth confession is made unto salvation"* (Rom. 10:9–10). *"For whosoever shall call upon the name of the Lord shall be saved"* (Rom. 10:13). By His grace, God has already done everything to provide salvation. Your part is simply to believe and receive.

Pray out loud: "Jesus, I acknowledge that I've sinned and need to receive what you did for the forgiveness of my sins. I confess that You are my Lord and Savior. I believe in my heart that God raised You from the dead. By faith in Your Word, I receive salvation now. Thank You for saving me."

The very moment you commit your life to Jesus Christ, the truth of His Word instantly comes to pass in your spirit. Now that you're born again, there's a brand-new you!

Please contact us and let us know that you've prayed to receive Jesus as your Savior. We'd like to send you some free materials to help you on your new journey. Call our Helpline: **719-635-1111** (available 24 hours a day, seven days a week) to speak to a staff member who is here to help you understand and grow in your new relationship with the Lord.

Welcome to your new life!

Receive the Holy Spirit

As His child, your loving heavenly Father wants to give you the supernatural power you need to live a new life. *"For every one that asketh receiveth; and he that seeketh findeth; and to him that knocketh it shall be opened… how much more shall your heavenly Father give the Holy Spirit to them that ask him?"* (Luke 11:10–13).

All you have to do is ask, believe, and receive!

Pray this: "Father, I recognize my need for Your power to live a new life. Please fill me with Your Holy Spirit. By faith, I receive it right now. Thank You for baptizing me. Holy Spirit, You are welcome in my life."

Some syllables from a language you don't recognize will rise up from your heart to your mouth (1 Cor. 14:14). As you speak them out loud by faith, you're releasing God's power from within and building yourself up in the spirit (1 Cor. 14:4). You can do this whenever and wherever you like.

It doesn't really matter whether you felt anything or not when you prayed to receive the Lord and His Spirit. If you believed in your heart that you received, then God's Word promises you did. *"Therefore I say unto you, What things soever ye desire, when ye pray, believe that ye receive them, and ye shall have them"* (Mark 11:24). God always honors His Word—believe it!

We would like to rejoice with you, pray with you, and answer any questions to help you understand more fully what has taken place in your life!

Please contact us to let us know that you've prayed to be filled with the Holy Spirit and to request the book *The New You & the Holy Spirit*. This book will explain in more detail about the benefits of being filled with the Holy Spirit and speaking in tongues. Call our Helpline: **719-635-1111** (available 24 hours a day, seven days a week).

Call for Prayer

If you need prayer for any reason, you can call our Helpline, 24 hours a day, seven days a week at **719-635-1111**. A trained prayer minister will answer your call and pray with you.

Every day, we receive testimonies of healings and other miracles from our Helpline, and we are ministering God's nearly-too-good-to-be-true message of the Gospel to more people than ever. So, I encourage you to call today!

About the Author

Andrew Wommack's life was forever changed the moment he encountered the supernatural love of God on March 23, 1968. As a renowned Bible teacher and author, Andrew has made it his mission to change the way the world sees God.

Andrew's vision is to go as far and deep with the Gospel as possible. His message goes far through the *Gospel Truth* television program, which is available to over half the world's population. The message goes deep through discipleship at Charis Bible College, headquartered in Woodland Park, Colorado. Founded in 1994, Charis has campuses across the United States and around the globe.

Andrew also has an extensive library of teaching materials in print, audio, and video. More than 200,000 hours of free teachings can be accessed at **awmi.net**.

Contact Information

Andrew Wommack Ministries, Inc.

PO Box 3333
Colorado Springs, CO 80934-3333
info@awmi.net
awmi.net

Helpline: 719-635-1111 (available 24/7)

Charis Bible College

info@charisbiblecollege.org
844-360-9577
CharisBibleCollege.org

For a complete list of all of our offices,
visit **awmi.net/contact-us**.

Connect with us on social media.